Specific Ski

Place Value

by
April Duff, M.Ed.
and
Leland Graham, Ph.D.

illustrated by
Janet Armbrust

Level 1

50 60 70 80 90 100

Publisher
Key Education Publishing Company, LLC
Minneapolis, Minnesota

CONGRATULATIONS ON YOUR PURCHASE OF A KEY EDUCATION PRODUCT!

The editors at Key Education are former teachers who bring experience, enthusiasm, and quality to each and every product. Thousands of teachers have looked to the staff at Key Education for new and innovative resources to make their work more enjoyable and rewarding. We are committed to developing educational materials that will assist teachers in building a strong and developmentally appropriate curriculum for young children.

PLAN FOR GREAT TEACHING EXPERIENCES WHEN YOU USE EDUCATIONAL MATERIALS FROM KEY EDUCATION PUBLISHING COMPANY, LLC!

About the Authors

Dr. Leland Graham is a former college professor, principal, and teacher, who was twice voted "Outstanding Teacher of the Year." The author of 55 educational books, Dr. Graham is a popular speaker and workshop presenter throughout Georgia and the USA, as well as a presenter for NSSEA (National School Supply & Equipment Association). Thousands of teachers have benefited from his workshops on reading, math, and improving achievement scores.

April Duff is a literacy support teacher for Even Start in Burke County, Georgia. She has a M.Ed. in reading, language and literacy education from Georgia State University and a B.S. in early childhood education from Georgia College and State University. She has also taught fourth grade and kindergarten, and has served as a IEP Reading and Math Specialist for grades 1–5. Ms. Duff lives in Georgia and enjoys reading and traveling.

Acknowledgments

The authors would like to acknowledge the assistance of the following educators: Jean Anderson and Barry Doran, Math Coordinators from DeKalb County School System, Decatur, Georgia, and David Park, proofreader.

Credits
Authors: April Duff, M.Ed. and Leland Graham, Ph.D.
Publisher: Sherrill B. Flora
Illustrator: Janet Armbrust
Project Director: Debra Pressnall
Editor: George C. Flora
Cover Design: Annette Hollister-Papp
Page Design and Layout: Swan Johnson
Cover Photographs: © Digital Vision® Ltd.
All rights reserved, © Photodisc

Key Education welcomes manuscripts and product ideas from teachers. For a copy of our submission guidelines, please send a self-addressed, stamped envelope to:

Key Education Publishing Company, LLC
Acquisitions Department
9601 Newton Avenue South
Minneapolis, Minnesota 55431

Standard Book Number: 1-933052-50-3
Specific Skills: Place Value — Level 1
Copyright © 2007 by Key Education Publishing Company, LLC
Minneapolis, Minnesota 55431

Table of Contents

Introduction

In *Specific Skills: Place Value* you will find a collection of reproducible math activities, pattern pages, and easy-to-play learning games to help students, especially struggling learners, develop an understanding of base-ten concepts and number quantities. Each book in this series also includes assessment opportunities in the form of a pretest/posttest, which has been formatted according to national standards. A special feature in this series is the "Place Value for Parents" letter. This reproducible handout incorporates math-related literature with fun at-home activities to further enhance each child's understanding of place value. The authors believe that the letter will also encourage parental involvement. Finally, provided in the back of each resource book is a list of Web sites that may be useful to teachers and parents. Some of the Web sites are information based, which will be helpful in designing lesson plans. Other Web sites offer place value games that children will enjoy playing while learning number concepts at the same time.

Specific Skills: Place Value—Level I is aligned with NCTM (National Council of Teachers of Mathematics) Standards. The practice pages and partner games can be used in a variety of ways, including whole group lessons, independent student work, or as enrichment activities at home. Based on various standards, the activities cover the following essential math skills:

- Naming and writing numerals 1–100
- Counting ones and tens
- Using expanded notation
- Ordering and comparing numbers
- Adding and subtracting two-digit numbers

Before place value concepts are introduced to young children, it is important that they have had adequate practice visualizing number quantities by working with concrete materials. To do this, it may be appropriate to provide the children with certain quantities of identical objects, such as drinking straws or toothpicks, and guide them as they count and arrange the items into bundles of 10. You might also consider having the children work with ten-frame grids (Toucan Ten-Frame Grids pattern on page 9). Provide either dried beans or large pasta rings for the children to use on the grids to show quantities up to 20. Later, as the children become proficient with this task, they may enjoy playing the games "Thirty to Win!" and "100 Puffy Pillows" (directions on page 48). As their level of understanding advances, challenge the children by having them build number quantities between 20 and 100 on multiple copies of the ten-frame grids as well as complete the activities on pages 12–18. This process of arranging sets of identical objects into groups of 10 with "some left over" is an important step to master. When children have internalized this concept, they should be able to identify quickly how many tens are part of numbers 10–30 and they will then be ready for more challenging tasks using base-ten models to complete the remaining games and activities offered in this book. Please keep in mind that some special needs children may benefit from working extensively with ten-frame grids instead of plastic, proportional base-ten models (rods and units) or paper models (ten-strips and squares), because they can construct number quantities 1–100 on the grids. If your students are experiencing success with ten-frame grids and are having difficulty with number-comparison activities on paper, you might consider directing those students to use the grids when deciding which sign—greater than, less than, or equal to—makes a number sentence true.

Pretest/Posttest A

Directions: Circle the correct answers.

---

1. Which word matches this number?

    # 7

    A. two   B. seven   C. ten

---

2. Which number matches this word?

    # thirteen

    A. 10   B. 13   C. 30

---

3. What number is shown?

    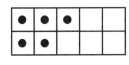

    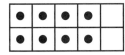

    A. 85   B. 58   C. 13

---

4. What is the number?

    # 3 tens + 4 ones

    A. 34   B. 304   C. 310

---

5. What number is shown?

    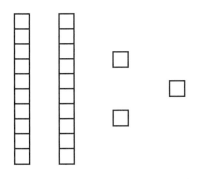

    A. 23   B. 113   C. 13

---

6. What is the number?

    # 20 + 5

    A. 52   B. 25   C. 205

Pretest/Posttest B

Directions: Circle the correct answers.

---

1. Which number comes next?

   # 65, 66, ___

   A. 67   B. 68   C. 64

2. Which number comes before?

   # ___, 42, 43

   A. 39   B. 41   C. 45

---

3. These numbers are in order from greatest to least. Fill in the blank.

   # 37, 35, ___, 30, 28

   A. 36   B. 29   C. 32

4. Choose the correct sign.

   # 132 ◯ 321

   A. >   B. <   C. =

---

5. What number is **10 less** than the number given?

   # 52

   A. 42   B. 51   C. 152

6. What number is **10 more** than the number given?

   # 37

   A. 32   B. 38   C. 47

Place Value for Parents

Dear Parents and Guardians,

In math class, your child will be learning about place value and comparing number quantities. To develop a sense about numbers, it is important for children to have rich math experiences with counting collections of objects (20–100 items) and arranging them into bunches of 10 with things "left over." The concept of place value is sometimes difficult for children to grasp. To help your child at home, please consider reading the following books and practicing the included activities together with your child:

MathStart®: A Fair Bear Share is written by Stuart J. Murphy and illustrated by John Speirs (HarperTrophy, 1998). This delightful story is about four bear cubs who must gather enough berries, seeds, and nuts so Mama Bear can bake her Blue Ribbon Blueberry Pie for dinner. As the story unfolds, the reader learns that not all cubs are eager to assist. The clever use of illustrations help children to see how making groups of 10 is a useful skill. Suggestions for fun math activities are also included.

Another book written by Stuart Murphy and illustrated by David T. Wenzel is *MathStart®: More or Less* (HarperTrophy, 2005). Find out how comparing numbers can be a lot of fun by reading this book. The story is about a young boy named Eddie who is blindfolded and sitting above a dunk tank at the Bayside School fair. His challenge is to guess correctly the age of people with only six or less questions. If not, he gets dunked! Eddie is quite clever and readers will enjoy learning about his strategies. Additional activity suggestions are also included in the book.

Activity: How Much Is One Hundred?
Materials Needed: toasted o-shaped cereal, pencil, and paper
Directions: Count out 10 small o's. Guess how many groups of 10 small o's would equal 100 small o's. If you wish to continue, have your child count out 100 small o's.

Activity: Exchanging Pennies for Dimes
Materials Needed: pennies and dimes
Directions: Gather enough pennies and dimes so your child can practice showing equivalent values, such as 20 pennies equal 2 dimes (20 cents), 30 pennies equal 3 dimes (30 cents), and so on. Make up various problems to practice this concept. Also talk about how many cents equal one dollar.

Thank you for your assistance,

Using Manipulatives and Hundreds Chart

Toucan Ten-Frame Grids

It is important for children to visualize number quantities. As an example of this, have each child fill in ten-frame grids (pattern on page 9) with pasta, buttons, or other small objects to show specific sets of numbers up to 20. The ten-frame game cards on page 57 can also be used to assess your student's understanding of base-ten concepts by having them identify the number represented on each card. *Note:* There are some cards that show only a few dots on each grid, such as the 5 + 5 card and the 3 + 7 card. If children incorrectly say that the numbers shown on those cards are 55 and 37, respectively, instead of 10, this may indicate that they still do not understand base-ten concepts.

For multisensory number experiences, provide Toucan Ten-Frame Grids flash cards for numbers 1–20 or higher with identical objects glued on them. To make a set of flash cards, glue the corresponding number of pasta shells, beans, or other objects onto copies of the grids that have been mounted on poster board. Have the children practice identifying the numbers randomly, counting by 10s to reach the totals.

Base-Ten Models

Be sure the children thoroughly understand what it means to make groups or bundles of 10 objects before using actual base-ten models (units and rods) to represent numbers greater than 30. If paper models are used, make copies of the patterns on page 49 and then have the children glue large pasta rings on them. It is much easier to recognize a group of ten items when groupings of five are shown in different colors. For example, the first five pasta rings may be blue and the remaining five rings may be red. Now the children can touch and count the individual "units" to build a solid understanding that the paper strip represents one group of 10.

1-100 Chart

The Count to 100! chart on page 10 can be used for many activities. Photocopy the chart for each student and choose from the following activities:

Even Numbers: Teach children that even numbers are 0, 2, 4, 6, and 8. Color those numbers **light blue**. Then tell the students that each number that has a 0, 2, 4, 6, or 8 in the ones place is also **even**. Ask students to help you pick out even numbers. Let the children color as many even numbers as they want. It may be necessary to discuss this concept several times; therefore, you may want to stop at 20 on the first day.

Odd Numbers: The odd numbers are 1, 3, 5, 7, and 9. Have the children color the odd numbers **pink**. Each number that has a 1, 3, 5, 7, or 9 in the ones place is also **odd**. Ask the students to help pick out the odd numbers. Let them color as many odd numbers as they want. Again, you may want to continue this activity over several days; therefore, pace the lesson accordingly.

Counting by 5s: Starting with 5, 10, 15, count to 100 with the children. Color these numbers **green**. Ask the students to count by 5s and identify those numbers that are even and those that are odd. Ask the children to look for the patterns.

Counting by 10s: Model counting by 10s for the children. Then have the students repeat the sequence with you several times. Color these numbers **orange**. Do they notice anything? All the multiples of 10 are already colored blue and green. Therefore, they are all even numbers because they have a "0" in the ones place!

Counting up to 100: Have the children cover their boards with 100 miniature marshmallows and then group them into sets of 10. Give each child 10 pillow bugs (pattern on page 52). Have them glue ten marshmallows (each group of five a different color) on each bug. If interested, use the pillow bugs when playing the game "100 Puffy Pillows."

Toucan Ten-Frame Grids

Directions on page 8

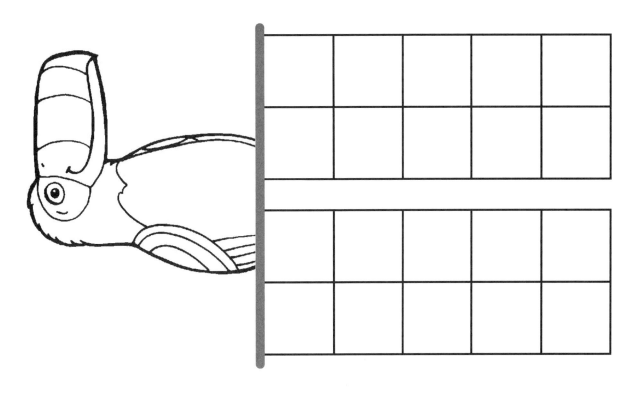

✂ –

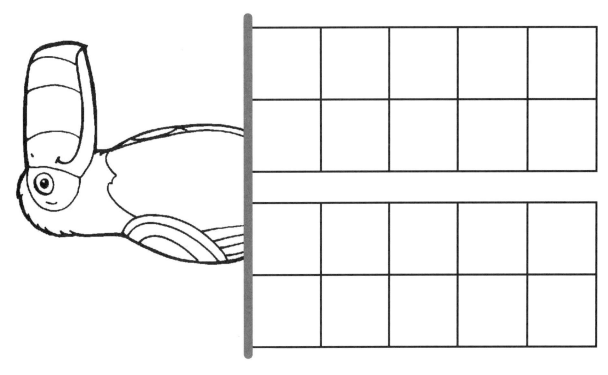

Count to 100!

Directions on page 8

1	2	3	4	5	6	7	8	9	10
11	12	13	14	15	16	17	18	19	20
21	22	23	24	25	26	27	28	29	30
31	32	33	34	35	36	37	38	39	40
41	42	43	44	45	46	47	48	49	50
51	52	53	54	55	56	57	58	59	60
61	62	63	64	65	66	67	68	69	70
71	72	73	74	75	76	77	78	79	80
81	82	83	84	85	86	87	88	89	90
91	92	93	94	95	96	97	98	99	100

Numeral Names

Directions: Write the numerals I to 9 on the cars. Write the number word in the blank. Draw the correct number of dots on each flag.

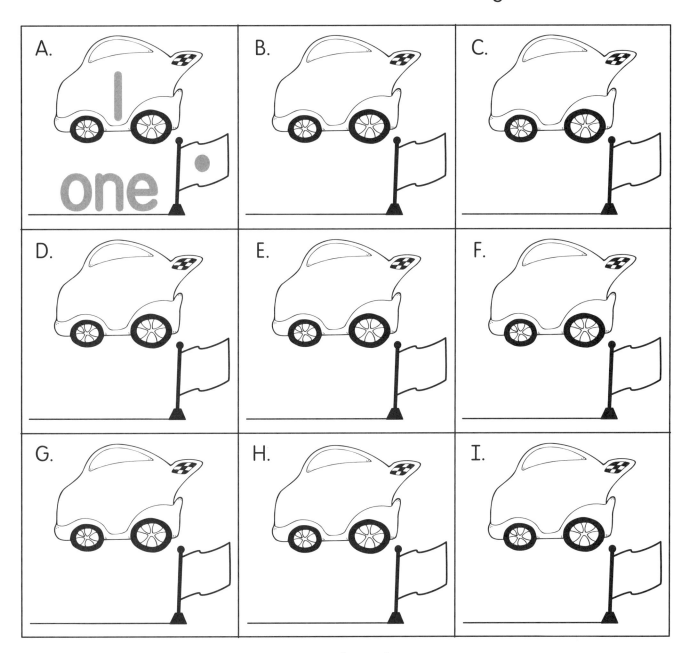

Word Bank

eight   five   four   nine   one

seven   six   three   two

Busy Bees in Hives

1. Count the bees below.

How many bees? _____

Draw a hive around 10 bees.

10 + _____ = _____

2. Count the bees below.

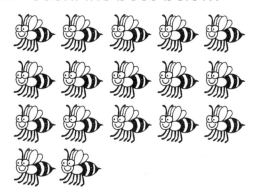

How many bees? _____

Draw a hive around 10 bees.

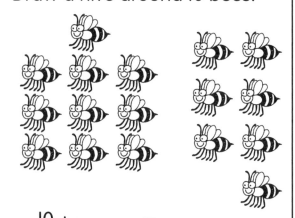

10 + _____ = _____

3. Count the bees below.

How many bees? _____

Draw a hive around 10 bees.

10 + _____ = _____

Shells in Buckets

Directions: Cut out the shells. Count and glue the shells on the buckets. Fill in the missing numbers.

18 = _____ + _____

11 = _____ + _____

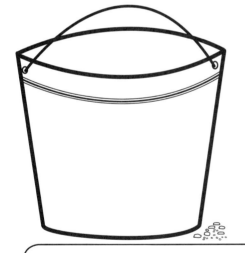

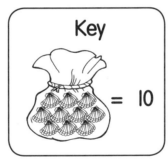

Key

= 10

14 = _____ + _____

16 = _____ + _____

 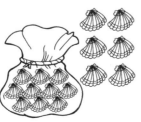 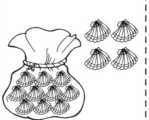 

Hands On: Use shell-shaped pasta to show the number sentences.

Buggy Numbers

Directions: Circle each group of 10 bugs.
Count the bugs in each set. Write the number in the blank.

A.

Number of bugs: _____

B.

Number of bugs: _____

C.

Number of bugs: _____

D.

Number of bugs: _____

E.

Number of bugs: _____

F.

Number of bugs: _____

Direction: Write the missing numbers on the lines.

$10 +$ _____ $= 15$ $10 +$ _____ $= 17$ $20 +$ _____ $= 21$

$10 +$ _____ $= 19$ $20 +$ _____ $= 26$ $20 +$ _____ $= 23$

Name _____   Date _____

How Many in All?

Directions: Draw a circle around each group of 10.
Fill in the missing numbers. See the example done for you.

A.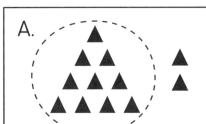

tens __1__   ones __2__   in all __12__

B.

tens ____   ones ____   in all ____

C.

tens ____   ones ____   in all ____

D.

tens ____   ones ____   in all ____

E.

tens ____   ones ____   in all ____

F. Draw your own picture.

tens __3__   ones __6__   in all ____

Diving into Numbers

Directions: Circle groups of 10 fish in each box. Count the fish. Write the tens and ones. Then write the total number of fish on the line.

Hands On: Draw lots of bubbles in the water. Then cover the bubbles with pasta rings. How many bubbles in all?

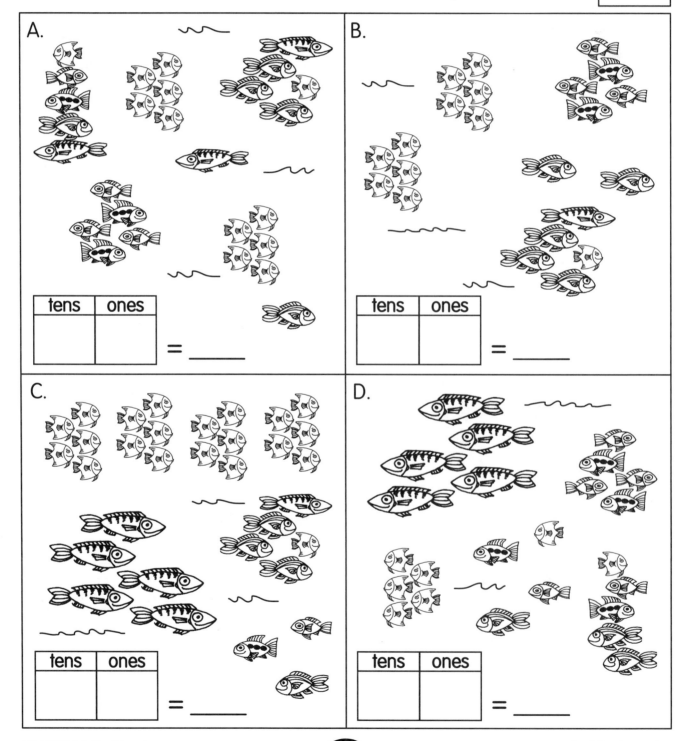

A.

tens	ones

= _____

B.

tens	ones

= _____

C.

tens	ones

= _____

D.

tens	ones

= _____

You Make the Picture!

Directions: Write the number on each blank. Make your own picture.

Example:

tens	ones
3	1

31 ___

1.

tens	ones
1	9

___

2.

tens	ones
3	7

___

3.

tens	ones
2	1

___

4.

tens	ones
3	5

___

5.

tens	ones
2	8

___

Tallying Up the Points

Directions: Draw the tally marks for each animal. Circle the groups of 10.

Direction: Write the given numbers in order from smallest to largest.

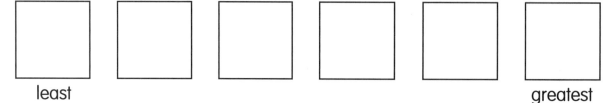

least   greatest

Number Recognition

Directions: Read the numbers. Use the chart to color the picture.

Blue (Light) — 0 to 10	**Green** — 31 to 40	**Orange** — 61 to 70
Yellow — 11 to 20	**Red** — 41 to 50	**Blue (Dark)** — 71 to 80
Purple — 21 to 30	**Black** — 51 to 60	**Pink** — 81 to 90

Counting Ones and Tens

Directions: Count the sets of blocks and write the numbers.

Example:	E.
Stands for ones: __4__ Stands for tens: __40__	
A.	**F.**
B.	**G.**
C.	**H.**
D.	**I.**

More Counting Ones and Tens

Directions: Write the tens and ones and then write the number on the line.

A.

tens	ones

_____

B.

tens	ones

_____

C.

tens	ones

_____

D.

tens	ones

_____

E.

tens	ones

_____

F.

tens	ones

_____

Direction: Write the above numbers in order from least to greatest.

_____   _____   _____   _____   _____   _____

least   greatest

Leapfrog!

Directions: Count by 10s. Write the numbers on the lily pads.

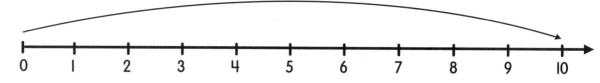

A.

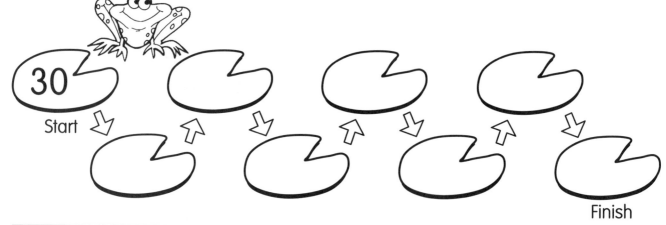

B.

C.

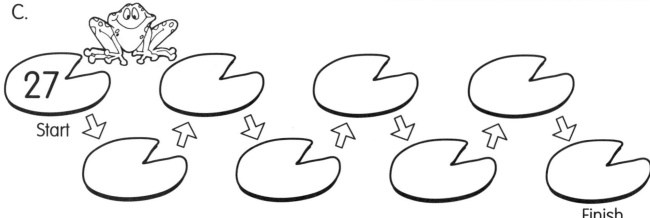

Expanded Notation

Directions: Write each number in expanded form.

Example: For the number fifty-eight,
the **standard form** is 58.
The **expanded form** is 5 tens + 8 ones.

A. 13 = _____ ten + _____ ones

B. 56 = _____ tens + _____ ones

C. 24 = _____ tens + _____ ones

D. 37 = _____ tens + _____ ones

E. 60 = _____ tens + _____ ones

F. 71 = _____ tens + _____ one

G. 95 = _____ tens + _____ ones

H. 86 = _____ tens + _____ ones

I. 20 = _____ tens + _____ ones

J. 42 = _____ tens + _____ ones

Number Riddle

Directions: Look at each problem. Write the number on the line.
Use the letter under each answer to solve the riddle.

1. I ten + 6 ones ___ B	2. I ten + 0 ones ___ Z	3. 2 tens + 0 ones ___ W
4. 2 tens + 3 ones ___ F	5. 2 tens + 9 ones ___ H	6. 3 tens + I one ___ U
7. 3 tens + 8 ones ___ Y	8. 4 tens + 3 ones ___ T	9. 5 tens + 7 ones ___ D
		10. 6 tens + 2 ones ___ N

Riddle: What did the ladybug say to the bee?

Answer:

___ ___ ___   ___ O ___ ' ___ ___   ___ O ___
20 29 38   57   62 43   38   31

___ ___ ___ ___   O ___ ___ !
16 31 10 10   23 23

Matching with Expanded Notation

Directions: Match the number or set of blocks to its expanded form.

34   =   30 + 4

Column A

Column B

1. 34

A. 30 + 7

2.

B. 40 + 9

3.

C. 60 + 6

4. 71

D. 30 + 4

5.

E. 10 + 0

6. 23

F. 40 + 3

7.

G. 20 + 3

8. 66

H. 70 + 1

What Comes Before or After?

Directions: Write the numbers that come **before**.

A. ____ , 13, 14	B. ____ , 19, 20	C. ____ , 25, 26
D. ____ , 31, 32	E. ____ , 44, 45	F. ____ , 67, 68

Directions: Write the numbers that come **after**.

G. 15, 16, ____ , ____	H. 20, 21, ____ , ____	I. 27, 28, ____ , ____
J. 38, 39, ____ , ____	K. 52, 53, ____ , ____	L. 75, 76, ____ , ____

What Comes Between?

Directions: Write the missing number in each blank.

A. 2, ____ , 4	B. 9, ____ , 11	C. 16, ____ , 18
D. 20, ____ , 22	E. 27, ____ , 29	F. 33, ____ , 35
G. 36, ____ , 38	H. 40, ____ , 42	I. 45, ____ , 47
J. 59, ____ , 61	K. 72, ____ , 74	L. 89, ____ , 91
M. 94, ____ , 96		

Greater Than, Less Than

Directions: Compare the sets. Write > or < in each circle.

1.	2.	3.
10 ◯ 8	15 ◯ 19	20 ◯ 30
4.	5.	6.
31 ◯ 25	28 ◯ 32	43 ◯ 36

Build It, Draw It!

Directions: Using base-ten blocks, show the following numbers. Draw pictures of your work. Write > or < in each circle.

A. 26 ◯ 18	B. 33 ◯ 41	C. 21 ◯ 12

More Greater Than, Less Than

Directions: Study each problem. Write >, <, or = in the circle.

Remember: > stands for *greater than*
< stands for *less than*
= means *equal to*

---

1. Compare the number of legs.

 ○

2.	3.	4.
12 ○ 10	23 ○ 32	35 ○ 35

5.	6.	7.
14 ○ 41	52 ○ 52	61 ○ 59

8.	9.	10.
74 ○ 58	80 ○ 80	88 ○ 93

Build It, Draw It!

Directions: Use base-ten blocks to make a number that is greater than 52.
Draw a picture to show your work.

52   <

Making New Numbers

Directions: Use the numbers on the cards to make new numbers.
Write them on the lines. Make each number sentence true.

Remember: **>** stands for *greater than*
< stands for *less than*

tens	ones
9	8

tens	ones
8	9

98 **>** 89

A.

tens	ones

tens	ones

_____ **<** _____

B.

tens	ones

tens	ones

_____ **<** _____

C.

tens	ones

tens	ones

_____ **>** _____

Ordering Numbers

Directions: Write the numbers in order from **least to greatest**.

A. 12 5 24 **5 12 24**	B. 27 22 17 _____	
C. 31 26 22 _____	D. 81 73 83 _____	E. 64 50 70 _____

Directions: Write the numbers in order from **greatest to least**.

F. 12 9 38 **38 12 9**	G. 23 33 28 _____	H. 24 19 20 _____
	I. 90 92 89 _____	J. 76 70 73 _____

Tic-Tac-Toe Place Value

Direction: Use the clues to play the game.
Circle the winning animal.

35	51	75
47	52	64
25	46	53

1. Draw an **O** around **5 tens 2 ones.**

2. Draw an **X** on **5 tens 3 ones.**

3. Draw an **O** around **7 tens 5 ones.**

4. Draw an **X** on **2 tens 5 ones.**

5. Draw an **O** around **3 tens 5 ones.**

6. Draw an **X** on **5 tens 1 one.**

7. Draw an **O** around **4 tens 7 ones.**

8. Draw an **X** on **4 tens 6 ones.**

Direction: Write the circled numbers in order from least to greatest.

_____   _____   _____   _____
smallest   largest

Ones and Tens – More or Less

Directions: Write the number that is **one more** than the number given.

A. 3 _____

B. 17 _____

C. 24 _____

D. 39 _____

Directions: Write the number that is **one less** than the number given.

E. 12 _____

F. 54 _____

G. 21 _____

H. 36 _____

Directions: Write the number that is **10 more** than the number given.

I. 15 _____

J. 33 _____

K. 26 _____

L. 48 _____

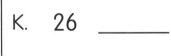

Directions: Write the number that is **10 less** than the number given.

M. 81 _____

N. 67 _____

O. 52 _____

P. 75 _____

Name That Number!

Directions: Using the numbers given, answer the following questions.

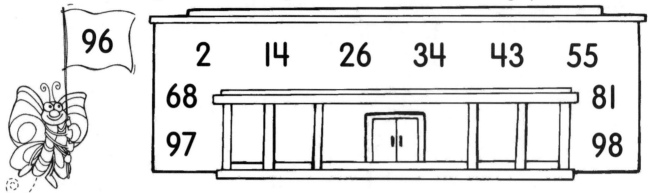

1. Which number has a **3** in the ones place and a **4** in the tens place?   _____

2. Which number is **10 less** than 24?   _____

3. Which number is between **67** and **69**?   _____

4. Which number has an **8** in the tens place?   _____

5. Which number is **10 more** than 16?   _____

6. Which number has a **4** in the ones place and a **3** in the tens place?   _____

7. Which number has the **same digit** in the ones and tens place?   _____

8. Which number is 3 less than 100?   _____

Numbers in Baskets

Directions: Solve each problem. Circle each group of 10. Count by 10s. Write the sum in the basket.

A.

B.

C.

D.

Direction: Write the sums in order from greatest to least.

_____   _____   _____   _____
largest   smallest

More Tic-Tac-Toe Place Value

Directions: Use the clues to play the game.
Circle the winning animal.

62	94	49
58	68	77
97	85	63

1. Draw an X on **9 tens 7 ones.**

2. Draw an O around **6 tens 8 ones.**

3. Draw an X on **4 tens 9 ones.**

4. Draw an O around **8 tens 5 ones.**

5. Draw an X on **7 tens 7 ones.**

6. Draw an O around **6 tens 3 ones.**

7. Draw an X on **9 tens 4 ones.**

8. Draw an O around **6 tens 2 ones.**

Direction: Write the circled numbers in order from greatest to least.

_____   _____   _____   _____
largest   smallest

Flying High with Numbers

Directions: Add to find the sums. Use the color key to color the picture.

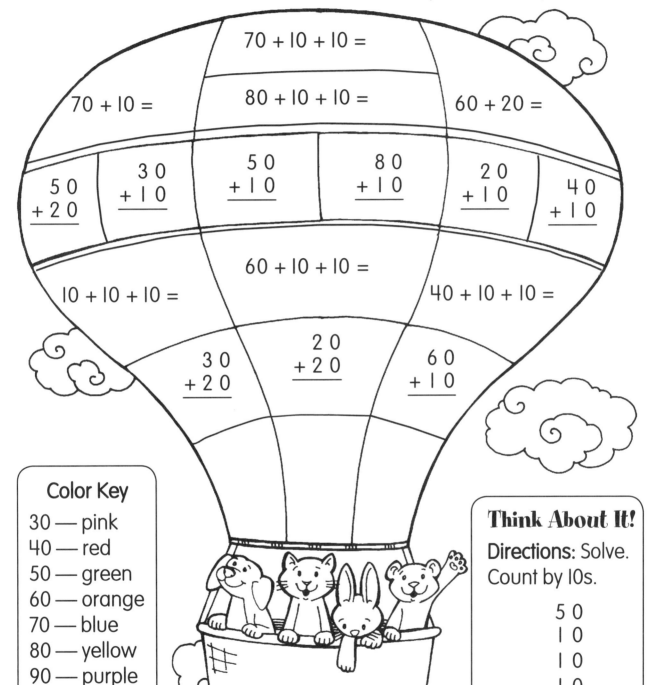

70 + 10 + 10 =

70 + 10 =

80 + 10 + 10 =

60 + 20 =

```
  5 0
+ 2 0
```

```
  3 0
+ 1 0
```

```
  5 0
+ 1 0
```

```
  8 0
+ 1 0
```

```
  2 0
+ 1 0
```

```
  4 0
+ 1 0
```

60 + 10 + 10 =

10 + 10 + 10 =

40 + 10 + 10 =

```
  3 0
+ 2 0
```

```
  2 0
+ 2 0
```

```
  6 0
+ 1 0
```

90 + 10 =

Color Key

30 — pink
40 — red
50 — green
60 — orange
70 — blue
80 — yellow
90 — purple
100 — brown

Think About It!

Directions: Solve.
Count by 10s.

```
  5 0
  1 0
  1 0
  1 0
+ 1 0
```

Ordering Numbers

Directions: Color by numbers! Use the code below:

- Blue — The numbers are in order from **least to greatest**.
- Green — The numbers are in order from **greatest to least**.
- White — The numbers are **not in order**.

22, 28, 32

7, 28, 18

12, 84, 40

80, 90, 12

63, 73, 83

36, 47, 48

46, 6, 88

98, 47, 50

45, 30, 24

4, 20, 7

67, 59, 35

48, 52, 99

32, 48, 57

82, 53, 37

82, 53, 37

70, 90, 100

22, 33, 44

103, 100, 95

60, 62, 71

108, 98, 56

19, 33, 57

Greater Than, Less Than, Equal To

Directions:
Compare the numbers.
Write >, <, or = in each circle.

Remember:
> stands for *greater than*
< stands for *less than*
= means *equal to*

A.
97 ◯ 87

B.
65 ◯ 100

(>)

C.
62 ◯ 91

D.
52 ◯ 52

E.
90 ◯ 99

(<)

F.
73 ◯ 95

G.
98 ◯ 86

H.
67 ◯ 67

I.
100 ◯ 80

(=)

39 *Specific Skills: Place Value*

Counting with Manipulatives

Directions: Add the sets of base-ten blocks in each problem. Write the sum on the bag. Then add 10 to the sum. Write the new number on the line.

A.   +   =   What number is 10 more?

_____

B.   +   =   What number is 10 more?

_____

C.   +   =   What number is 10 more?

_____

D.   +   =   What number is 10 more?

_____

E.   +   =   What number is 10 more?

_____

Make It! Draw It!

Directions: Use base-ten blocks to solve the problems. Draw pictures of your work on the back of this page.

F. $16 + 20 =$ _____

G. $31 + 20 =$ _____

H. $54 + 20 =$ _____

Name _____ Date _____

Adding with Manipulatives

Directions: Use base-ten models.
Solve each problem.

A.	1 ten 2 ones	plus	1 ten 3 ones	= _____
B.	1 ten	plus	2 tens 4 ones	= _____
C.	8 ones	plus	2 tens	= _____
D.	3 tens 5 ones	plus	2 tens 2 ones	= _____
E.	3 tens 2 ones	plus	3 tens 4 ones	= _____
F.	4 tens 6 ones	plus	2 tens 3 ones	= _____
G.	3 tens 7 ones	plus	2 tens 2 ones	= _____

Make It! Draw It!

Directions: Use base-ten blocks to add the numbers. Draw pictures of your work on the back of this page.

H. 27 and 14   I. 35 and 15   J. 56 and 16

More Adding with Manipulatives

Directions: Use base-ten models.
Solve each problem.

A.	1 ten 7 ones	plus	3 tens 2 ones	= _____
B.	4 tens	plus	3 tens 6 ones	= _____
C.	6 ones	plus	6 tens 2 ones	= _____
D.	3 tens 3 ones	plus	5 tens 4 ones	= _____
E.	5 tens 5 ones	plus	4 tens 3 ones	= _____
F.	6 tens 4 ones	plus	3 tens 3 ones	= _____
G.	2 tens 8 ones	plus	7 tens 1 one	= _____

Make It! Draw It!

Directions: Use base-ten blocks to make addition problems for these sums.
Draw pictures of your work on the back of this page.

H. 21   I. 50   J. 63

Name _____   Date _____

Adding with Place Value Chart

Directions: Add to find the sum.

A.

tens	ones
1	1
+	6

B.

tens	ones
2	3
+	5

C.

tens	ones
9	0
+	6

D.

tens	ones
7	1
+	8

E.

tens	ones
2	6
+ 1	3

F.

tens	ones
2	4
+ 2	4

G.

tens	ones
5	0
+	4

H.

tens	ones
3	2
+ 1	3

I.

tens	ones
3	5
+ 2	1

Subtracting with Manipulatives

Directions: Use base-ten models.
Solve each problem to find the difference.

A.	3 tens 2 ones	minus	1 ten	= _____
B.	1 ten 3 ones	minus	2 ones	= _____
C.	2 tens 7 ones	minus	1 ten 5 ones	= _____
D.	3 tens 3 ones	minus	3 ones	= _____
E.	4 tens 6 ones	minus	1 ten 3 ones	= _____
F.	3 tens 5 ones	minus	2 tens 5 ones	= _____
G.	3 tens 8 ones	minus	3 tens 2 ones	= _____

Make It! Draw It!

Directions: Use base-ten blocks. Write subtraction sentences. Draw pictures of your work on the back of this page.

H. 50 minus 13   I. 30 minus 15   J. 40 minus 11

More Subtracting with Manipulatives

Directions: Use base-ten models.
Solve each problem.

A.	6 tens 9 ones	minus	2 tens 5 ones	= _____
B.	6 tens 4 ones	minus	3 tens 4 ones	= _____
C.	4 tens 9 ones	minus	2 tens 3 ones	= _____
D.	9 tens 5 ones	minus	6 tens 2 ones	= _____
E.	8 tens 6 ones	minus	3 tens 2 ones	= _____
F.	9 tens 2 ones	minus	7 tens 1 one	= _____
G.	7 tens 8 ones	minus	1 ten 7 ones	= _____

Make It! Draw It!

Directions: Use base-ten blocks. Make subtraction problems.
Draw pictures of your work on the back of this page.

H. ___ – ___ = 17   I. ___ – ___ = 32   J. ___ – ___ = 54

Subtracting with Place Value Chart

Directions: Subtract to find the difference.

A.		
	tens	ones
	1	3
−		2

B.		
	tens	ones
	2	5
−	1	0

C.		
	tens	ones
	2	8
−	1	5

D.		
	tens	ones
	3	2
−	1	2

E.		
	tens	ones
	9	7
−	3	4

F.		
	tens	ones
	4	7
−	2	0

G.		
	tens	ones
	5	6
−	2	5

H.		
	tens	ones
	5	1
−	4	1

I.		
	tens	ones
	6	8
−	3	3

Place Value and Money

To the teacher: One fun way to teach place value is by using money. For these activities, provide 100 pennies and 10 dimes. Copy the cards onto colored card stock. If interested, have the children complete the activities in the math center.

Activity 1

Ten pennies equal one dime.

If you had 30 pennies,
how many dimes would that equal?

_____ dimes

Activity 2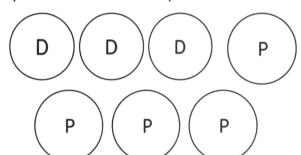

Trade pennies for dimes. Give your partner 5 dimes. How many pennies should you get back?

5 dimes = _____ pennies

Now make up your own problems.

Activity 3

When we add pennies and dimes, we are adding cents (¢).

Add:

$$\begin{array}{r} 2 \text{ dimes} \quad 3 \text{ pennies} \\ + \ 4 \text{ dimes} \quad 2 \text{ pennies} \\ \hline \text{___ dimes ___ pennies} \end{array}$$

or _____ ¢ in all

Activity 4   Place dimes (D) and pennies (P) on the pictures below.

D   D   D   P

P   P   P

How many cents in all? _____ ¢

Activity 5

Subtract:

$$\begin{array}{r} 7 \text{ dimes} \quad 5 \text{ pennies} \\ - \ 3 \text{ dimes} \quad 3 \text{ pennies} \\ \hline \text{___ dimes ___ pennies} \end{array}$$

or _____ ¢

Activity 6

Pretend you are at a candy store.
Buy a chocolate candy for 23¢.
You pay with 3 dimes.
How much change will you get?

30¢ – 23¢ = _____ ¢

Directions for Partner Games

Thirty to Win!

Materials Needed
- standard die
- game board pattern (page 51)
- 65 game pieces (dried beans or pasta pieces)

Getting Ready
- Reproduce copies of the game board onto colored paper. Make one game board for each player.
- Set aside about 65 game pieces.

How to Play
First have the players determine who starts. Then direct the players to take turns rolling the die, collecting the corresponding number of game pieces, and placing them in the ones columns on their game boards. When a group of 10 is made, those game pieces are then moved onto one of the ten-frame grids. At the end of each round, the players must announce their total number of pieces in order to keep the new pieces. If the number is incorrect, that player loses the game pieces that were just collected. The first player to collect a total of 30 or more pieces wins the game.

100 Puffy Pillows

Materials Needed
- die pattern A (page 50)
- game patterns (pages 52 and 53)
- colored miniature marshmallows
- glue, scissors, and lightweight cardboard

Getting Ready
- Reproduce a copy of the bed and 10 pillow bugs onto card stock for each player.
- Glue the pillow bugs onto lightweight cardboard and cut out. Glue 10 marshmallows on the body of each pillow bug to give it a dimensional shape.
- Reproduce die pattern A onto card stock. Cut out the die shape along the dashed lines. Fold on the solid lines. To make the cube, glue the flaps, as indicated, underneath the outer panels.

How to Play
Each player is given a "bed." Place 20 pillow bugs in the center of the playing area. Have the players take turns rolling the die and collecting the matching number of pillow bugs, which are then placed on the "beds." At the end of each round, the players count by 10s the number of "pillows" on their game board and announce their totals. If the total is incorrect, that player returns the pillow bugs that were just collected. The first player to collect "100 puffy pillows" wins the game.

Tubful of Tens

Materials Needed
- die patterns A and B (page 50)
- game board pattern (page 54)
- 20 craft sticks and a box of large pasta rings
- glue and scissors

Getting Ready
- Reproduce a game board for each player onto card stock.
- Glue 10 pasta rings on each craft stick to make a "bubble stick."
- Make the dice by following the directions provided for the game "100 Puffy Pillows."

How to Play
Give each player a game board. Place the bubble sticks and about 50 pasta rings ("bubbles") in the center of the playing area. To start the game have each player roll die B. The player who rolls the larger number begins the first round. Direct the players to take turns rolling both dice and collecting the matching number of bubble sticks and bubbles (pasta rings). When a group of 10 bubbles is made, the player exchanges those bubbles for a bubble stick and then arranges the bubble sticks on the tub. At the end of each round, the players announce their totals. If the total is incorrect, that player puts back the bubbles that were just collected. The game ends when the first player has gathered "100 or more bubbles."

Capture the Treasure!

Materials Needed
- game board pattern (page 55)
- toucan number cards (pages 58 and 59)
- scissors

Getting Ready
- Reproduce the game board pattern and number cards onto colored card stock. Cut along the dashed lines to separate the game pieces.

How to Play
Arrange the toucan number cards facedown in the center of the playing area. Each player chooses a treasure chest. Have the players take turns drawing a number card. If the number comes between the two numbers shown on the player's game board, the card is kept by that player and set on the treasure chest. If the card cannot be used, it is placed in the discard pile. The players continue taking turns by drawing cards. The first player to collect four cards captures the treasure! Have the players exchange game boards and play again.

Number Safari

Materials Needed
- 2 game markers
- game board pattern (page 56)
- game cards — ten-frame grids (page 57)
- game cards — number cards (pages 58 and 59)
- base-ten model patterns (shown below)
- 220 pasta shapes or beans
- lightweight cardboard, scissors, and glue

Getting Ready
- Make a copy of the game board on colored card stock paper.
- Duplicate two copies of the cards on page 57. Make one copy of the cards on pages 58 and 59. Use card stock if desired.
- Make 10 rods (ten-strips) and 10 units (squares) for each player. Reinforce the models by gluing them onto lightweight cardboard and then cutting them out. Glue pasta pieces in the individual boxes.

How to Play
Number Safari: Name the Number! — Scatter the ten-frame cards facedown in the center of the playing area. Each player chooses a game marker and places it on "Start" on the game board. Have the players take turns drawing a card and identifying the number quantity shown. If the answer is correct, the player advances two spaces for an even number or three spaces for an odd number. Place the card in the discard pile. The first player to land on "Stop!" wins the game.

Number Safari: Write It, Build It! — Arrange the toucan number cards facedown in the playing area. Have each player choose a game marker and place it on "Start" on the game board. Direct the players to take turns drawing a toucan card and reading the number aloud for the partner. The other player then writes that given number on a piece of paper and builds it with the place value models. That player advances one space for the written number (if correct) and one space for the number set (if correct) on the game board. The game continues until a player lands on "Stop!" and wins the game.

Base-Ten Model Patterns (Ten-Strip and Squares)

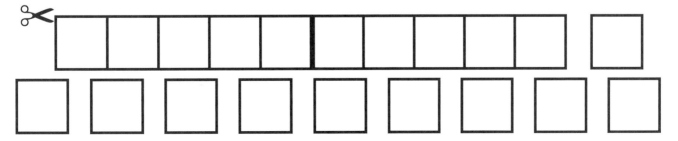

Game directions on page 48

Die A

+20

Glue here.

+10

Add
1 ten.

+10

Add
2 tens.

Glue here.

Glue here.

+10

Die B

+3

Glue here.

+6

+5

+4

+5

Glue here.

Glue here.

+7

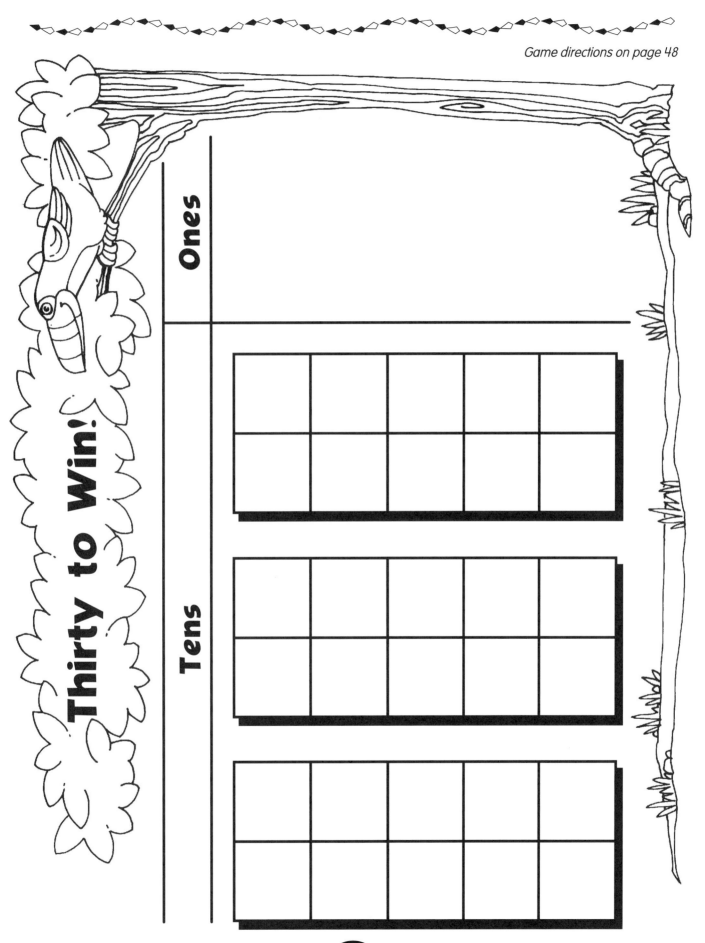

Thirty to Win!

Ones

Tens

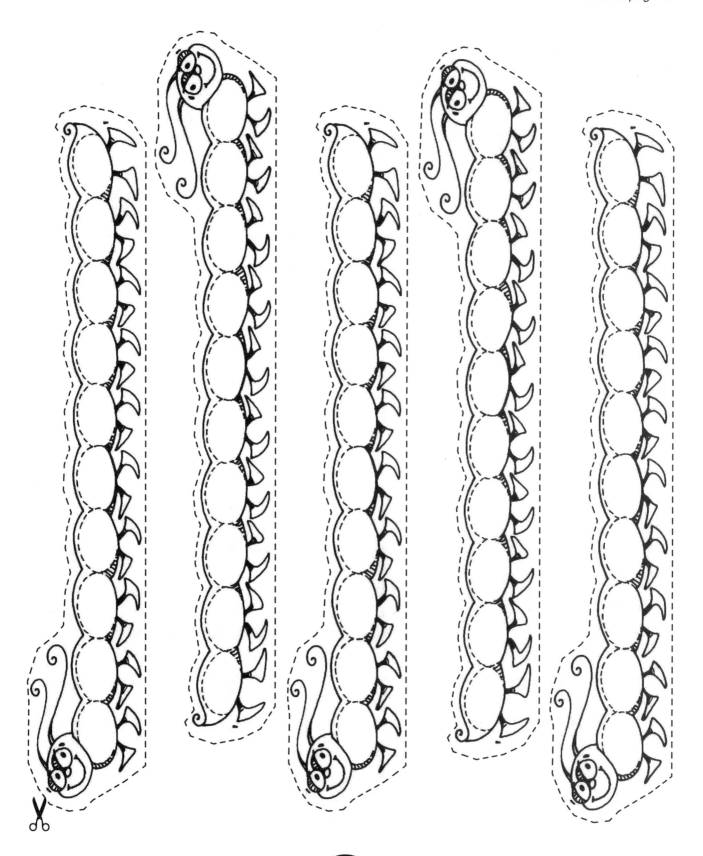

Game directions on page 48

100 Puffy Pillows

54 *Specific Skills: Place Value*

Capture the Treasure!

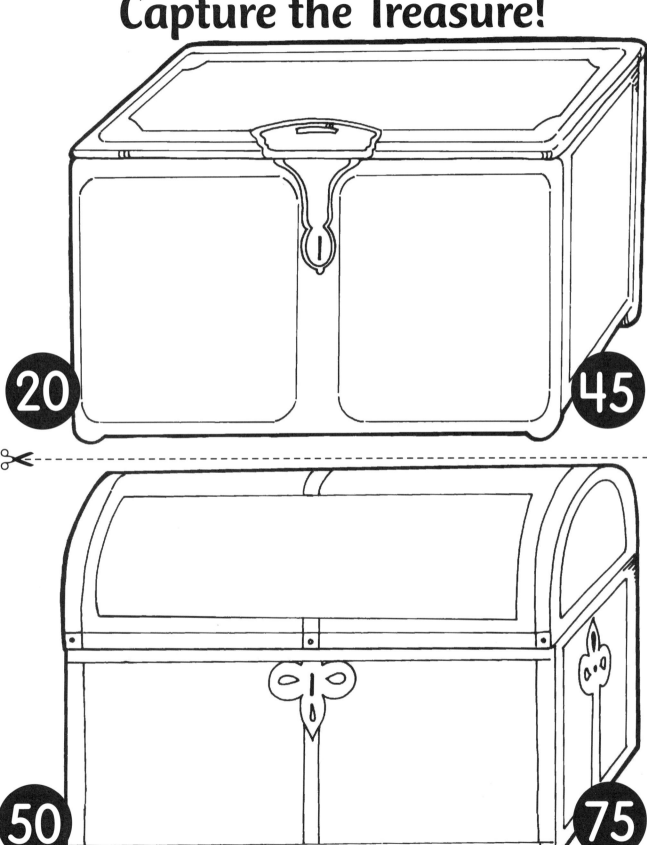

Game directions on page 49

Number Safari

Land on "Stop!" to win.

Stop!

Slide back.

Move up 3 spaces.

Start

Walk across.

**Capture the Treasure/
Number Safari: Write It, Build It!**

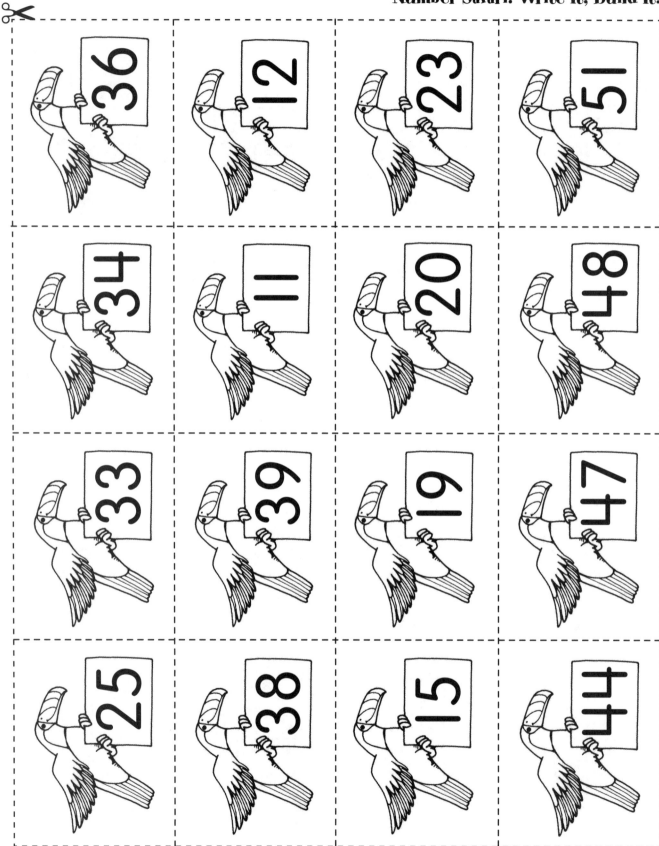

58

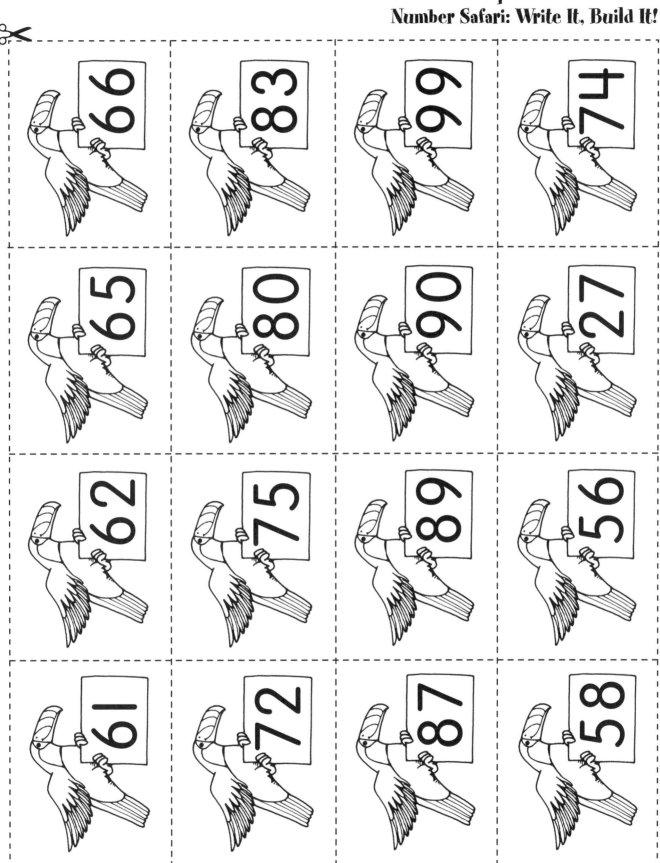

To the teacher: Copy the flash cards onto colored card stock. Cut them out for use in a math center.

Name the value of the underlined digit.

14

Name the value of the underlined digit.

47

Name the value of the underlined digit.

62

Add the cards. What is the number?

90   6

Name the value of the underlined digit.

83

Add the cards. What is the number?

70   9

To the teacher: Copy the flash cards onto colored card stock. Cut them out for use in a math center.

What place is the **2** in?

What place is the **5** in?

What place is the **4** in?

Add the cards. What is the number?

What place is the **6** in?

Add the cards. What is the number?

Web Sites

http://www.hbschool.com/activity/count/index.html

Children can practice writing numbers by playing the game "Count Along to 100." To play the game just fill in the missing numbers on a hundreds chart.

http://www.dositey.com/addsub/tenoneex.htm

For those children who need additional practice identifying ones and tens, they can count the pictures and write the number in the box.

http://www.gamequarium.com/placevalue.html

This Web site offers a listing of different place value games. For students, the following games and exercises may be appropriate: "Collect Ten" (ten-frame grids), "Base Ten Blocks," and "Place Value Lesson: Tens and Ones."

http://www.learningbox.com/Base10/CatchTen.html

To play "Catch Ten," the player must click on the base-ten unit cubes as they float down the river. BT Bear stands ready to catch those blocks. When he has enough to make a strip of ten, he will toss the blocks on shore and then wait to catch some more.

http://www.edhelper.com/place_value.htm

Internet (printable) worksheets for teachers and parents can be found at this site.

http://www.arcytech.org/java/b10blocks/

This site offers a great interactive place value screen for kids. Be sure to click on the "name" button first to learn about each feature.

http://www.eduplace.com/math/mathsteps/2/a/

This site has a good explanation of place value for teachers and parents to use as a reference. This site also offers "tips and tricks" and suggestions for how to answer your students' questions.

http://mathforum.org/library/drmath/sets/elem_place_value.html

Dr. Math is the best! You can use this site for all kinds of math questions, and of course, Dr. Math answers place value questions.

Answer Key

Page 5
I. B, 2. B, 3. C, 4. A, 5. A, 6. B

Page 6
I. A, 2. B, 3. C, 4. B, 5. A, 6. C

Page II
A. I, one, one dot; B. 2, two, two dots; C. 3, three, three dots; D. 4, four, four dots; E. 5, five, five dots; F. 6, six, six dots; G. 7, seven, seven dots; H. 8, eight, eight dots; I. 9, nine, nine dots

Page 12
I. 12, 10 + 2 = 12; 2. 17, 10 + 7 = 17; 3. 13, 10 + 3 = 13

Page 13
18 = 10 + 8; 11 = 10 + 1; 14 = 10 + 4; 16 = 10 + 6

Page 14
A. 15, B. 21, C. 17, D. 19, E. 26, F. 23
Bottom of page: 10 + 5 = 15; 10 + 7 = 17; 20 + 1 = 21; 10 + 9 = 19, 20 + 6 = 26; 20 + 3 = 23

Page 15
B. I, 8, 18; C. I, 7, 17; D. 2, 0, 20; E. 2, 5, 25
F. 36; Drawings will vary.

Page 16
A. 2 tens, 7 ones, 27; B. 2 tens, 2 ones, 22; C. 3 tens, 3 ones, 33; D. 2 tens, 4 ones, 24

Page 17
Check student's drawings.

Page 18
Check student's tally marks.
Bottom of page: 23, 30, 36, 44, 48, 55

Page 19
Check student's coloring.

Page 20
A. 2, B. 5, C. 7, D. 9, E. 10, F. 30, G. 40, H. 60, I. 90

Page 21
A. I ten, 4 ones, 14; B. 3 tens, 8 ones, 38; C. 5 tens, 6 ones, 56; D. 3 tens, 2 ones, 32; E. 8 tens, 0 ones, 80; F. 7 tens, 2 ones, 72;
Bottom of page: 14, 32, 38, 56, 72, 80

Page 22
A. 30, 40, 50, 60, 70, 80, 90, 100
B. 14, 24, 34, 44, 54, 64, 74, 84
C. 27, 37, 47, 57, 67, 77, 87, 97

Page 23
A. I ten, 3 ones; B. 5 tens, 6 ones; C. 2 tens, 4 ones; D. 3 tens, 7 ones; E. 6 tens, 0 ones; F. 7 tens, I one; G. 9 tens, 5 ones; H. 8 tens, 6 ones; I. 2 tens, 0 ones; J. 4 tens, 2 ones

Page 24
I. 16, 2. 10, 3. 20, 4. 23, 5. 29, 6. 31, 7. 38, 8. 43, 9. 57, 10. 62
Riddle: Why don't you buzz off!

Page 25
I. D, 2. E, 3. F, 4. H, 5. B, 6. G, 7. A, 8. C

Page 26
A. 12; B. 18; C. 24; D. 30; E. 43; F. 66; G. 17, 18; H. 22, 23; I. 29, 30; J. 40, 41; K. 54, 55; L. 77, 78

Page 27
A. 3, B. 10, C. 17, D. 21, E. 28, F. 34, G. 37, H. 41, I. 46, J. 60, K. 73, L. 90, M. 95

Page 28
I. >, 2. <, 3. <, 4. >, 5. <, 6. >
Bottom of page: A. >, B. <, C. >
Check student's models.

Page 29
I. >, 2. >, 3. <, 4. =, 5. <, 6. =, 7. >, 8. >, 9. =, 10. <
Build It, Draw It! Check student's model.

Page 30
A. 67 < 76; B. 24 < 42; C. 53 > 35

Answer Key

Page 31
B. 17, 22, 27; C. 22, 26, 31; D. 73, 81, 83; E. 50, 64, 70; G. 33, 28, 23; H. 24, 20, 19; I. 92, 90, 89; J. 76, 73, 70

Page 32
Numbers with O: 35, 75, 47, 52
Numbers with X: 51, 25, 46, 53
The cat is circled.
Bottom of page: 35, 47, 52, 75

Page 33
A. 4, B. 18, C. 25, D. 40, E. 11, F. 53, G. 20, H. 35, I. 25, J. 43, K. 36, L. 58, M. 71, N. 57, O. 42, P. 65

Page 34
1. 43, 2. 14, 3. 68, 4. 81, 5. 26, 6. 34, 7. 55, 8. 97

Page 35
A. 36, B. 78, C. 57, D. 49
Bottom of page: 78, 57, 49, 36

Page 36
Numbers with O: 62, 68, 85, 63
Numbers with X: 94, 49, 77, 97
The bear is circled.
Bottom of page: 85, 68, 63, 62

Page 37
Answers across the balloon:
Row 1: 90
Row 2: 80, 100, 80
Row 3: 70, 40, 60, 90, 30, 50
Row 4: 30, 80, 60
Row 5: 50, 40, 70
Basket: 100
Think About It! Answer: 90
Check student's coloring.

Page 38

Check student's coloring.

Page 39
A. >, B. <, C. <, D. =, E. <, F. <, G. >, H. =, I. >

Page 40
A. 25, 35; B. 49, 59; C. 37, 47; D. 48, 58; E. 30, 40
F. 36; G. 51; H. 74

Page 41
A. 25, B. 34, C. 28, D. 57, E. 66, F. 69, G. 59
Bottom of page: Check student's models.

Page 42
A. 49, B. 76, C. 68, D. 87, E. 98, F. 97, G. 99
Check student's models.

Page 43
A. 17, B. 28, C. 96, D. 79, E. 39, F. 48, G. 54, H. 45, I. 56

Page 44
A. 22, B. 11, C. 12, D. 30, E. 33, F. 10, G. 6
Bottom of page: Check student's models.

Page 45
A. 44, B. 30, C. 26, D. 33, E. 54, F. 21, G. 61

Page 46
A. 11, B. 15, C. 13, D. 20, E. 63, F. 27, G. 31, H. 10, I. 35

Page 47
1. 3 dimes; 2. 50 pennies; 3. 6 dimes, 5 pennies, 65¢; 4. 34¢; 5. 4 dimes, 2 pennies, 42¢; 6. 7¢